The Thames Valley

Nick Channer

COUNTRYSIDE BOOKS
NEWBURY BERKSHIRE

First published 2007
© Nick Channer, 2007

COUNTRYSIDE BOOKS
3 Catherine Road
Newbury, Berkshire

To view our complete range of books,
please visit us at
www.countrysidebooks.co.uk

ISBN 978 1 84674 013 8

Photographs by the author

*Cover picture of the Thames Valley at
Winter Hill was supplied by
Pictures of Britain (Raymond Lea)*

Designed by Peter Davies, Nautilus Design
Maps by Gelder Design & Mapping

Produced through MRM Associates Ltd, Reading
Typeset by CJWT Solutions, St Helens
Printed by Cambridge University Press

Contents

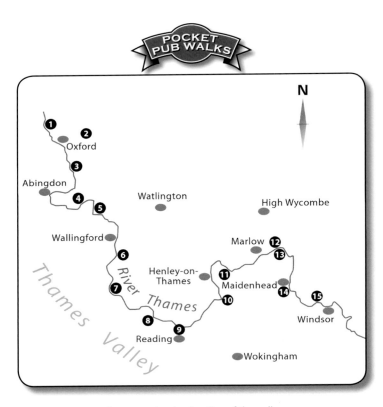

Area map showing location of the walks

Introduction

When we think of the gentle beauty of southern England, we tend to picture rolling beechwoods, chocolate-box villages and lush watermeadows. It may be a somewhat romanticised image but broadly it captures the essence and character of our unique, unspoiled landscape. One crucial feature of this intricate, finely detailed canvas is the River Thames, Britain's most famous river and a waterway whose name and distinctive beauty are known and appreciated throughout the world.

The valley, through which this glorious river journeys on its way to the sea, is equally delightful and either side of the Thames there are numerous opportunities to explore miles of undulating countryside on foot. The walks in this book cover the Thames Valley between Oxford and Windsor and here you can learn all about the region's fascinating literary associations, its long and colourful history and its rich architectural heritage. For example, Walk 2 at Headington Quarry takes you to the grave of renowned literary scholar C.S. Lewis, Walk 12 passes the former home of children's writer Enid Blyton, Walk 5 reveals the treasures of historic Dorchester Abbey, and Walk 9 explores the ancient, lesser-known corners of Reading.

Almost all the walks include at least one stretch of Thames riverbank and here your route coincides with the 180-mile Thames Path, one of Britain's newest national trails. A walk by this enchanting river is a journey in more ways than one. Today, the Thames is really no more than a recreational linear park but in previous centuries it played a very prominent role as a vital trade and communications route. Follow the Thames Path and you'll find the river's story is told on information boards at regular intervals along the way. The Thames has often been described as 'liquid history' and there is no better label. This really is a journey into the past.

As well as providing a window on the region's history and stunning beauty, these circular routes, which vary between 2 and 6½ miles in length, offer ideas and suggestions for other things to do in the area before or after completing the walk. Useful information and telephone numbers are provided. One of the classic ingredients for an enjoyable walk in the country is a good pub and all the routes start and finish at or very near a classic hostelry. Details of food, ales and opening times are featured. If using the pub car park while doing the walk, please consult the landlord first – and you should, of course, be a customer.

Happy walking in the Thames Valley!

Nick Channer

Publisher's Note

We hope that you obtain considerable enjoyment from this book; great care has been taken in its preparation. However, changes of landlord and actual closures are sadly not uncommon. Likewise, although at the time of publication all routes followed public rights of way or permitted paths, diversion orders can be made and permissions withdrawn.

We cannot, of course, be held responsible for such diversion orders and any inaccuracies in the text which result from these or any other changes to the routes nor any damage which might result from walkers trespassing on private property. We are anxious though that all details covering the walks are kept up to date and would therefore welcome information from readers which would be relevant to future editions.

The simple sketch maps that accompany the walks in this book are based on notes made by the author whilst checking out the routes on the ground. However, for the benefit of a proper map, we do recommend that you purchase the relevant Ordnance Survey sheet covering your walk. The Ordnance Survey maps are widely available, especially through booksellers and local newsagents.

The Trout Inn

Ancient history and the natural beauty of the landscape are this walk's perfect bedfellows. Just a few hundred yards from the start are the remains of Godstow Nunnery. According to legend, the body of Fair Rosamund, the beautiful mistress of Henry II, was buried here after she had been poisoned by the formidable Eleanor of Aquitaine. At least that is the popular version of the story. Nothing was ever proved and in reality, Rosamund may well have simply died of old age, after retiring to Godstow to become a nun. The nunnery was eventually dissolved in the mid-16th century. During the

Distance – 5½ miles.

OS Explorer 180 Oxford, Witney & Woodstock. GR 484093.
Wonderfully atmospheric walk beside the Thames with views across Oxford's ancient grazing land. Return along the towpath of the Oxford Canal.

Starting point The large pub car park opposite the Trout at Wolvercote.

How to get there Follow the A34 round the west side of Oxford and exit at the Pear Tree roundabout. Head south on the A44 to the next roundabout, then turn right for Wolvercote. Follow the road through the village, pass a public pay and display car park on the left and continue to the Trout. Its car park is on the right opposite the pub.

Civil War it was garrisoned for Charles I but seized in 1646 and virtually destroyed by order of the Puritan commander, Colonel Fairfax. The middle stages of the walk are dominated by views of Port Meadow, a 345-acre area of common and grazing land where the Freemen and Commoners of Oxford can graze geese, cattle and horses. This ancient tradition even gets a mention in the Domesday survey of 1086.

THE PUB Dating back to about 1133, the **Trout Inn** was originally a hospice serving Godstow Nunnery. The pub has a distinguished history – Matthew Arnold and Lewis Carroll knew it and Colin Dexter describes it as a 'fine riverside hostelry' in his Inspector Morse novel *The Jewel That Was Ours*. On offer are various snacks and freshly cut sandwiches – fillings include rump steak and red onion jam, honey roast ham and mature cheddar, smoked salmon and cream cheese and chargrilled chicken. Classic main courses range from toad-in-the-hole and roasted stuffed aubergine to beef and Bass pie and chicken Monte Cristo. Scampi, Cajun swordfish steak, calves' liver and bacon and gammon steak are among other options. Adnams and Bass feature as real ales and Stella Artois is also available at the bar.

Open 11 am to 11 pm every day.
☎ *01865 302071*

1 On leaving the pub turn left and cross the **Thames**. On the far side turn left again to join the route of the **Thames Path**, signposted '**Osney**'. The timeless Oxford skyline – 'that sweet city with her dreaming spires' as the 19th-century poet Matthew Arnold described this great seat of learning – is glimpsed almost

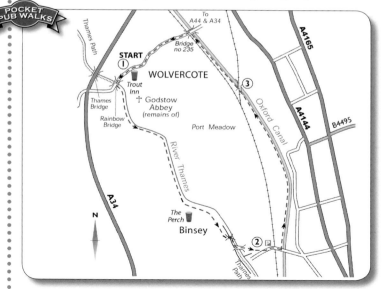

The River Thames, with Port Meadow beyond.

immediately. Pass the remains of **Godstow Nunnery** and walk along to **Godstow Lock**. Here you are treated to the first views of **Port Meadow** on the opposite bank of the river. Continue alongside the Thames, pass through several gates and at length you reach a path signposted to the **Perch Inn**. Depending on your need for rest and refreshment at this point on the walk, turn right here for the pub or keep ahead on the towpath. Go through more gates to reach **Bossom's Boatyard** and just beyond it cross **Rainbow Bridge**, restored in 1997. Turn right and keep lines of moored boats on the left.

2 Swing left at the next bridge where you will find a public footpath sign. Walk to the edge of **Port Meadow**, avoid a path running off to the right just beyond the bridge and curve right on the stony path. Go through several gates on the far side to join a road and walk ahead. Cross the railway and at the junction with **William Lucy Way**, turn right to join the towpath of the **Oxford Canal**. Swing sharp left on reaching it after a few paces and pass under **bridge 242**. Continue on the towpath. Pass some reed beds

with interpretive boards and keep ahead beneath a modern brick bridge. Recently built residential developments crowd in along this stretch of the walk and an assortment of narrow boats – some brightly coloured, some in a dilapidated state – adds to the intricate picture. Pass a swing bridge – **number 238** – and continue with sports facilities on the opposite bank.

3 Walk beneath a railway bridge and keep a railway line close by you on the left. Look for **bridge 236** and head for **235** and **Wolvercote Lock** beyond it. Turn left here, up a flight of steps to the road. Bear right at the top, cross the railway bridge and on the left is another fine view of **Port Meadow**. Avoid a bridleway running off to the left and a footpath to **Wolvercote Common** and head for **Wolvercote Post Office**. Keep left at a green beyond it and bear left opposite the **Red Lion pub**. Follow **Godstow Road** along to a large car park with toilet facilities and further along the road is a striking memorial to two members of the Royal Flying Corps who met their deaths in a monoplane accident near here in 1912. Continue along the road and shortly you reach the **Trout** where the walk started.

Place of interest nearby

Woodstock is famous for **Blenheim Palace**, England's largest stately home. The architect John Vanbrugh was commissioned to design the house for John Churchill, 1st Duke of Marlborough, following his victory over the French at Blenheim in 1704. Inside are various staterooms and tapestries, the Long Room, and the room where Winston Churchill was born. Nearby is **Bladon church** where the great statesman and his family are buried. Contact Woodstock Tourist Information Centre for further details. ☎ *01993 813276.*

2 **Horspath**

The Queen's Head

This **fascinating and richly varied** figure-of-eight walk
explores some of the splendid countryside on Oxford's
doorstep. After crossing Shotover Plain, the route heads for
the village of Headington Quarry, one of the city's lesser-known
gems. Make for the churchyard and here you'll find the much-
visited grave of the novelist and literary scholar C.S. Lewis – in
his lifetime one of Oxford's best-known residents. To see inside
the church, with its impressive Narnia window featuring Aslan
the Lion and the pew where Lewis and his brother worshipped,
contact the Vicarage on 01865 762931

Distance – 5¼ miles.

OS Explorer 180 Oxford, Witney & Woodstock.
GR 573048.
Very varied walk running across Shotover Plain on the rural
fringes of Oxford. There are several quite lengthy ascents
– one on the way to Shotover Plain and one on the way
back to it from Headington Quarry.

Starting point The Queen's Head, Horspath.

How to get there Horspath is about 1 mile to the east of the
Oxford ring road. Follow the A4142 to Cowley and then take
the Horspath road into the village. Turn left as the road bears
right by the green and then go immediately right into Church
Road. The inn is on the right. For those not patronising the
pub, there is alternative parking at Shotover Plain.

THE PUB

The **Queen's Head** dates back about 300 years and its stone
façade sits well among Horspath's picturesque cottages and
period houses. On the menu are various sandwiches and
toasties, a range of jacket potatoes and baguettes, and a choice
of more substantial dishes, such as bangers and mash, chicken
curry, and ham, egg and chips. Steak, Guinness and mushroom
pie is one of the pub favourites, and there is a traditional roast
on Sunday.

*Open Monday 5 pm to 11 pm; Tuesday, Wednesday and
Thursday from 12 noon to 3 pm and 5 pm to 11 pm; Friday
and Saturday between 12 noon and 11 pm; Sunday from
12 noon until 10.30 pm.*
☎ *01865 875567*

1 From the pub turn right and follow **Church Road**. Pass the village school and **Butts Road** and continue along **Blenheim Road**, following it through a predominantly residential area of Horspath. Further on the road surface gives way to potholes and stones as you leave the village to begin to climb between trees. Pass one of the entrances to **Shotover Country Park** on the left and continue climbing – quite steeply at this stage. Emerge from the woodland on reaching the high ground and follow the track between fields and hedgerows to a junction by a small reservoir. Turn left at the right of way sign. Pass a map of **Shotover Plain**, together with information about the area, and avoid the bridleway on the left at this point. Continue on the broad track running across Shotover Plain and eventually you reach a parking area with a transmitter just beyond it.

2 Cross the car park and follow the road ahead. There are fine views down towards the sprawling city of **Oxford** from this high

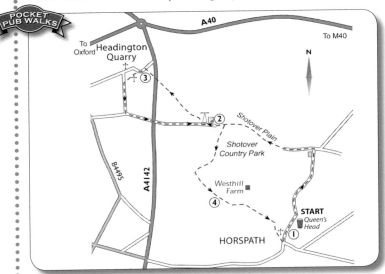

ground. Begin to drop down through the trees towards the mast and immediately beyond it turn right at the footpath sign. Follow the path through the trees and then through two gates. Continue between trees and farmland, avoiding turnings off, and along this stretch of the walk you begin to hear the rumble of traffic on the busy A4142. Make for a fork with a stile between the two paths,

Holy Trinity church at Headington Quarry.

keep left into the field and pass a galvanised kissing gate on the right. Keep on the grassy path over to the right, with a line of houses and gardens alongside it.

3 Cross the dual carriageway with care – there is an island to make the crossing easier – and continue on the path beside wooden panel fencing. On reaching a new housing development of stone and brick properties, turn left and follow the obvious enclosed path to a road in **Headington Quarry**. Cross it and continue on **Masons Alley** to reach the **Masons Arms** in the centre of the village. Bear left and then right after several steps at the sign for **Trinity Road**. Head for **Holy Trinity church**, pass to the left of it and look for the sign pointing to the **grave of C.S. Lewis**.

It was in 1948 that Lewis completed the first draft of The Lion, the Witch and the Wardrobe, *the first of the now legendary Narnia novels. He read it to his friend and fellow scholar J.R.R. Tolkien who apparently hated it. Lewis and Tolkien were members of a group called The Inklings and, between 1939 and 1962, they met every Tuesday morning at the Eagle and Child pub in Oxford to discuss, among other topics, the mythical elements of their work.*

Exit the churchyard by a gate and follow the enclosed path along to **Quarry Road**. Turn left, then left again at the T-junction and make for the bridge over the A4142. Head uphill to the car park for **Shotover Country Park**. Keep ahead to the far end of the car park, then turn right into woodland, immediately bearing left for a few paces to reach a bridleway junction. Turn right and follow the broad path gently downhill through the trees. Avoid turnings either side and continue ahead when you see the huge Cowley car plant ahead. Pass several houses, cross the drive leading to them, and turn immediately left at a sign, 'cyclists keep to bridle path'. Walk through the extensive woodland and then cross a tarmac track on a left-hand bend.

4 Follow the bridleway ahead across several fields, with **Westhill Farm** over to the left. As you draw level with it you will see the path curving left in the field corner. Exit the pasture at this point through a gap on the right and go out across the field towards the houses of **Horspath**. On the far side, pass through a gate and follow a path to a junction. Keep left, skirt some barns and stone cottages and at the road turn right. Walk along to the junction in the centre of the village, turn left into **Church Road** and return to the pub.

Places of interest nearby

Shotover Country Park covers 280 acres of wild countryside. Until the mid-17th century it was a royal hunting forest. The south-facing hillsides and small valleys make it a popular haunt for a variety of habitats. Nearby **Brasenose Wood** to the south-west offers excellent conditions for about 250 breeding pairs of birds, including the nightingale and the lesser-spotted woodpecker.

3 Sandford-on-Thames

The King's Arms

We all know the River Thames, Britain's greatest river. At least, we think we do. After all, it is as famous as fish and chips, Big Ben and the red London bus. Many of us have glimpsed it from a moving car or plied its waters as part of a cruise but how many people have witnessed the unique beauty and ever changing character of this most English of rivers from the Thames Path National Trail? This long-distance route follows the Thames from its source to the capital and offers unrestricted access to the water's edge almost all the way.

Starting from picturesque Sandford Lock, this fine riverside walk offers a taste of what it is like to stroll for miles beside the Thames, often with only wildlife and the occasional fellow walker for company.

The Thames Valley

THE PUB The recently refurbished **King's Arms** dates back to the 15th century and at one time much of the building was a successful papermill. Today, one of the pub's great attractions is its location overlooking Sandford Lock on the Thames. There are few riverside settings as attractive as this. Inside you can choose from an extensive menu that includes such dishes as halibut, lamb rump and fish cakes. There are also jacket potatoes, baguettes and various other snacks if you prefer lighter fare. The King's Arms also has a summer barbecue area in the garden. Courage Best and Directors are among the beers and there is also a choice of guest ales.

Open from 11 am to 11 pm on Monday to Saturday and from 11 am to 10.30 pm on Sunday.
☎ *01865 777095*

Distance – 6½ miles.

OS Explorer Explorer 180 Oxford, Witney & Woodstock and 170 Abingdon, Wantage & Vale of White Horse. GR 532012.
A pleasant walk to Radley College and then back along a very peaceful stretch of the Thames.

Starting point The King's Arms at Sandford-on-Thames.

How to get there *From the Oxford ring road make for the A4074 and then turn off for Sandford-on-Thames. From the A34, follow the A423 and the A4142, then turn right near Littlemore for Sandford, or follow the A4074 between the A423 and Wallingford and turn off for Sandford. In the village turn into Church Road and follow it to the pub.*

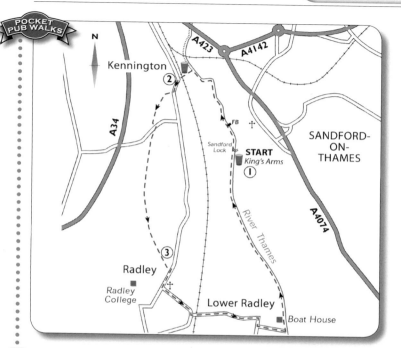

1 From the pub, cross adjacent **Sandford Lock** and turn right. Keeping the river on your right on this stretch of the walk, pass through a gate and cross a weir. Go over the next bridge and continue to the next footbridge. Follow the sign for **Oxford** and soon you skirt a meadow, still with the **Thames** on your right.

The Thames Path has come a long way since the 1920s when the idea of establishing a formal right of way along the entire length of the river was first mooted, though it wasn't until 1989 that the route was officially designated. Running from a Gloucestershire meadow to the Thames Barrier at Woolwich and officially opened by the Countryside Commission in the summer of 1996, the Thames Path is 180 miles long and takes up to three weeks to complete on foot.

The River Thames near Sandford Lock.

When you draw level with a large house identified by gables on the opposite side of the river, begin to veer away from the water, passing beneath pylon cables. Follow the outline of the path to a galvanised gate, cross a path by a cattle grid and take the footbridge across the railway.

2 Pass through the car park of a pub called the **Tandem** and turn left at the main road. Follow it to a roundabout and here turn right into **Bagley Wood Road**. Follow this narrow lane between houses and bungalows and continue to a waymarked path running to the left of a dwelling. Take it, pass between a fence and a wall and soon you rejoin the road. At the junction go straight across, following the path signposted to **Radley**. Keep right at the immediate fork and, on reaching a gate with a circular walk disc, keep ahead along the right-hand edge of the sports field. Aim for the right-hand corner, passing through a kissing gate between stone pillars. The names of local men killed in action during the Second World War can be seen on the reverse

side. Go straight on down a wide, grassy ride running between the trees, head for a wrought-iron kissing gate and a footbridge, cross a stream and walk straight ahead at the immediate junction of paths. Go up a slight incline, merge with another path and avoid a path on the right.

3 On reaching the road, go straight over to join a field path running to **Radley**. With the school buildings ahead, pass alongside woodland and take the alternative path through the trees as you approach double gates. Take the signposted path through the wood, with playing fields over to the right. Pass tennis courts and swing right to follow a broad track before reaching an enclosed path leading to the road. On reaching it, turn right and pass the main entrance to **Radley College**. Turn into **Church Road**, then left again for **Lower Radley**. Cross the railway and when the road bends right, head straight on for the **Thames Path**. Turn left at the sign for **Radley College Boathouses** and make for the riverbank. Turn left and head upstream for just under 2 miles. This stretch of the walk is largely quiet and uninhabited. At length you reach **Sandford Lock**. Cross over and return to the **King's Arms**.

Places of interest nearby

Oxford has much to interest the walker. In order to see everything this world-famous city has to offer, you would need to go back again and again. As well as the colleges, there are many other historic buildings and ancient monuments. **Christ Church Meadow**, the **University Botanic Garden**, the **Sheldonian Theatre** and the **Bodleian Library** are just a few of the many fascinating landmarks to be found within Oxford's boundaries. For more details, contact the Tourist Information Centre.
☎ *01865 726871.*

The Barley Mow

With such a famous and historic pub marking the start and finish of this Thamesside walk, you could be forgiven for thinking that the route itself might be something of an anti-climax. Not so. Just a few hundred yards from the Barley Mow, high on a bluff on the far side of the Thames, stands Clifton Hampden's church of St Michael and All Angels, designed by Sir George Gilbert Scott who, in the 1860s, conceived the plans for the Gothic six-arched river bridge crossed at the start and finish of the walk. Scott, who was

Distance – 2 miles.

OS Explorer 170 Abingdon, Wantage & Vale of White Horse. GR 548953.
Short, easy walk beside the Thames to Clifton Lock and then across farmland back into Clifton Hampden

Starting point The large car park opposite the Barley Mow in Clifton Hampden.

How to get there Take the A415 between Abingdon and Dorchester and turn off at Clifton Hampden, heading south in the direction of Long Wittenham. Cross the Thames and then turn left into the pub car park.

also responsible for the Albert Memorial and St Pancras railway station in London, allegedly sketched out the design on a shirt cuff. Locally-made coarse bricks were used to build it.

Beyond Clifton Lock the walk passes within sight of another well-known landmark in this corner of Oxfordshire, though one that is not as pleasing on the eye. Didcot Power Station can be seen from many vantage points in the Thames Valley and there are those who think it blends comfortably into the landscape – creating an unusual, even endearing, mix of natural and man-made features.

THE PUB

No reputable guide to the Thames would fail to mention the **Barley Mow**, immortalised in Jerome K. Jerome's literary classic *Three Men in a Boat*, published in 1889. In the book, Jerome describes the pub as 'the quaintest, most old-world inn up the river'. Its picturesque thatched roof, oak panelling and flagstoned public bar add to the charm, but take care with the low beams and doorways. Before the nearby bridge was built, crossing the Thames was by ferry. The toll-bridge keeper and

The Thames Valley

the ferryman before him used to sit in the inglenook fireplace and keep an eye out for approaching customers through the pub window. Salmon hollandaise, mixed grill, lamb foreshank and chicken forestière are among a range of popular dishes on the menu, and there is always of choice of sandwiches and baguettes for the hungry hiker. Ales are changed on a regular basis.

Open 12 noon to 11 pm (Sunday 10.30 pm).
☎ *01865 407847*

1 From the car park across the road from the **Barley Mow**, turn right and follow the road round to the left. Cross the bridge over the **Thames** and continue for a few paces to a path running sharp left down to the towpath. Turn right and keep the river beside

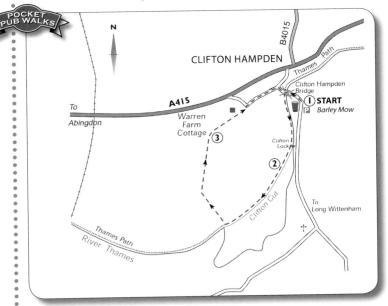

Pretty cottages in Clifton Hampden.

you on the left. Along this stretch are several signs relating to mooring fees. Keep ahead with other walkers and fleets of cabin cruisers for company. After some time you pass through a gate and beside **Clifton Lock** – note the date, 1929, on the front of the cottage.

2 Continue ahead to a pedestrian bridge; don't cross it but keep going on the towpath. Soon the familiar cooling towers of **Didcot Power Station** loom into view on the horizon. Follow the **Clifton Cut** ahead and just before you reach the end of a line of bushes on the left, turn right at the fence corner and walk along the right-hand perimeter of the field to a gap in the

hedge. Continue along a grassy track, rather overgrown in places at certain times of the year, with the boundary hedge on your left. Once more the power station is visible – closer this time, the unmistakable cooling towers just a few fields away. On the far side of the field the track broadens to reach a line of trees. Keep ahead on the dirt track in the next field, following it as it sweeps right and passes alongside clumps of trees and bushes.

3 Pass a 'no vehicular access' sign and follow the track between margins of nettles and bushes. Pass **Warren Farm Cottage** on the left, noting its charming garden, and follow the track, keeping to the right of farm outbuildings. The surface underfoot is now concrete. Go to the right of a large timber building and at the road turn right. On reaching a junction, with **Clifton Hampden church** opposite, turn right, re-cross the **Thames** bridge and return to the pub and car park.

Places of interest nearby

The **Pendon Museum** at Long Wittenham reproduces in miniature scenes of the English countryside around 1930 – an evocative but accurate depiction of a bygone age. Exquisitely modelled cottages, farms, fields and chalky lanes recall the quiet charm of the Vale of the White Horse. The museum also houses many fascinating railway relics, as well as a reconstruction of a small GWR signal box.
☎ *01865 407365.*

5 Dorchester

The Fleur de Lys

Drive into **Dorchester-on-Thames** for the first time and what strikes you immediately is its charm and character. With its pretty chocolate-box cottages, winding streets and quaint pub, it is the quintessential English village. What confirms this is Dorchester's appearance from time to time in the highly successful ITV drama *Midsomer Murders*. All the locations used in the series capture the beauty and spirit of the Thames Valley and the Home Counties.

The Thames Valley

Just across the way from the start of this attractive walk is historic Dorchester Abbey, which stands on the site of the first Saxon cathedral in Wessex. The building may be old but the history of the village goes back much further. The Romans built an important town known as Dorocina here, though its ramparts are now only faintly recognisable.

THE PUB The **Fleur de Lys** is a 600-year-old former coaching inn and one of the best known hostelries and buildings in the area. Eagle-eyed viewers of *Midsomer Murders* will probably recognise the exterior. Brakspear, Adnams and Hook Norton feature as real ales, while the menu offers sandwiches and baguettes as well as fresh fish, steak and traditional Sunday roast – among other dishes.

Open 12 noon until 11 pm (10.30 pm on Sunday).
☎ *01865 340502*

Distance – 3½ miles.

OS Explorer 170 Abingdon, Wantage & Vale of White Horse. GR 578941.
Pleasant, very easy walk to the banks of the Thames with the option to extend the route to the famous viewpoint on Castle Hill – a steep but rewarding climb.

Starting point The free parking area in Bridge End, Dorchester.

How to get there *From Oxford or Wallingford take the A4074, turn off at the signs for Dorchester and make for Bridge End opposite the Abbey. The Fleur de Lys is just a few minutes' walk along the main street.*

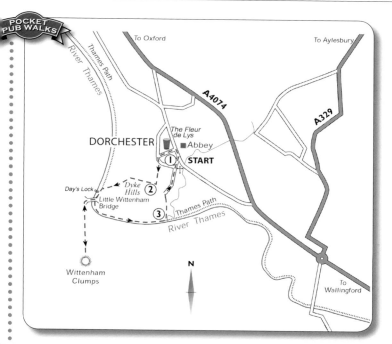

POCKET PUB WALKS

To Oxford

To Aylesbury

River Thames

Thames Path

A4074

A329

DORCHESTER

The Fleur de Lys

Abbey

START

①

Day's Lock

Dyke Hills ②

Little Wittenham Bridge

③ Thames Path

River Thames

Thames Path

Wittenham Clumps

N

To Wallingford

1 From **Bridge End** in the centre of **Dorchester** head back to the road, passing a telephone box and a former pub on the right before the junction. The old brewery sign outside is a clue. Keep left, with **Dorchester Abbey** on your right, and pass **Dorchester Antiques**.

The late John Betjeman said that the abbey was 'splendid in its proportions and details', while the Right Reverend Robert Runcie, Archbishop of Canterbury between 1980 and 1991, referred to it as 'a building which keeps alive our sense of the sacred in a busy world'. Inside the abbey are a number of treasures, including a 12th-century lead font decorated with figures of 11 apostles seated beneath a Romanesque arcade.

Dorchester was used as a location for Midsomer Murders.

Just before the **Fleur de Lys**, swing left into **Rotten Row**. Walk between lines of cottages and at the far end turn right to join a gravel path. Very soon the walk passes between allotments before reaching a junction with a gravel track by some cottages. Turn left and then keep left at a tarmac lane before leaving the road surface after a few paces at a willow tree to begin following the path signposted to **Day's Lock**. Abruptly, you are on the edge of Dorchester with fields and trees forming the backdrop. Head for the **Dyke Hills** ahead and at the obvious path junction in front of the embankment, turn right.

2 Cross a track by a notice that reads 'track to farm only' and keep on the path, which begins gradually to curve to the left. Continue to a gate and cross several meadows to reach a footbridge near **Day's Lock**. Cross the river to **Lock House Island** and head for **St Peter's church** at **Little Wittenham**. Turn left just beyond it, opposite the entrance to the manor,

keep right at the fork and head for the viewpoint on **Castle Hill** where there are tremendous vistas over the Thames Valley and beyond. Retrace your steps to **Day's Lock**, follow the towpath under the footbridge and keep the river beside you on the right. Pass through a gate beneath the branches of a tree and keep ahead to a galvanised gate. Continue ahead on the riverbank with a delightful curtain of woodland on the opposite bank.

3 As you begin to approach the next bridge, turn left and follow the path across meadows towards **Dorchester**. Make for a kissing gate, pass the remains of an old pillbox before reaching the next gate and in the next field keep right to a track by several houses and cottages. Follow **Wittenham Lane** back to **Bridge End** and the **Fleur de Lys**.

Places of interest nearby

Wallingford is blessed with some fine buildings and a long and fascinating history. The town has always been an important crossing point on the Thames, and it was Alfred the Great who fortified Wallingford against Danish attack. There is a museum in the High Street illustrating the town's rich heritage. For more information, contact the Tourist Information Centre.
☎ *01491 826972.*

The Perch and Pike

The name **Clara Butt** may not mean much to today's generation of promenaders who raise the roof at the Last Night of the Proms, but this concert and operatic contralto's memorable rendition of Elgar's classic *Land of Hope and Glory* made a lasting impression on audiences in the early years of the 20th century. Dame Clara lived at North Stoke, one of the features of this glorious riverside walk, and her grave can be found in the village churchyard. A mile or so to the west is the final resting place of another Dame of the British Empire – Agatha Christie. Britain's greatest crime writer lived at Winterbrook near Wallingford and she is buried at Cholsey. Christie's love of trains and railway travel is well known and the locally famous foot

Distance – 5 miles.

OS Explorer 171 Chiltern Hills West, Henley-on-Thames & Wallingford. GR 598834.
Attractive riverside walk initially following the route of the Ridgeway beside the Thames to North Stoke. The return leg is over cycle tracks and field paths.

Starting point The Perch and Pike car park or in the immediate vicinity of the pub.

How to get there South Stoke lies just off the B4009 north of Goring. Follow the A4074 between Reading and Wallingford and turn off at the signs for South Stoke. The pub is in the village centre, near the church.

tunnel beneath the railway near South Stoke evokes an air of mystery that could easily belong in one of her many detective novels. As you pass through the tunnel on your way back to the start of the walk, you may find yourself speculating as to whether Christie was inspired by this atmospheric stretch of track in her work.

The walk links South Stoke and North Stoke by following a peaceful stretch of the Thames upstream on the Ridgeway long-distance national trail, one of the south's most popular paths, which runs for 85 miles between Ivinghoe Beacon in Buckinghamshire and Avebury in Wiltshire. The return leg of the circuit is across open fields with views to distant downland.

THE PUB Everyone in this part of the Thames Valley has heard of the **Perch and Pike** at South Stoke. Only a few minutes from the river, this ancient hostelry has been serving drinks since the 17th century. The pub has many attractive features inside and adjacent to it is a 42-seater restaurant housed in a barn conversion. Food ranges from sandwiches to smoked haddock and salmon fishcakes. For meat lovers there is venison with celeriac mash and Madeira jus — among many other appetising dishes. Brakspear beers are on offer for real ale drinkers.

Open 12 noon until 3 pm and 6 pm until 11 pm from Monday to Saturday and 12 noon until 5 pm on Sunday.
☎ *01491 872415*

---

1 From the **Perch and Pike** turn right and walk along the village street, passing the primary school and church. At the junction

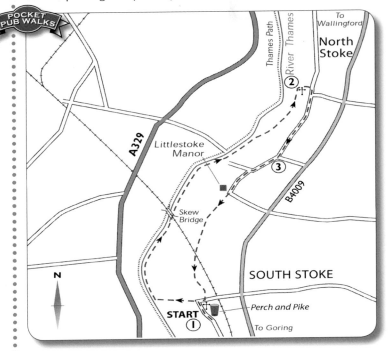

The attractive riverside walk follows the route of the Ridgeway at South Stoke.

veer left at the **Ridgeway** sign, keep left at the next Ridgeway signpost and walk along to the **Thames bank**. When you get there, turn right and head upstream with the river on your left, passing beneath Brunel's striking railway bridge, built in 1840 and known as the **Skew Bridge**. This intriguing, listed structure has a very distinctive atmosphere. Stand by the water's edge, look up and you can see the line above. As you linger on the towpath, you may suddenly hear a roar and a rumble as a train clatters along the track above you, the bridge echoing eerily to the sound of it. Continue on the **Ridgeway** to an attractive Georgian house with shutters. Just near it is a cottage. Follow the waymarks, still keeping the river on your left, and head for the church at **North Stoke**.

The Thames Valley

2 Pass through the churchyard; as you do so, look for the grave of Dame Clara Butt on your right. From the church gate follow the lane to the T-junction and turn left for a few steps to look at the rather unusual early 20th-century village hall. Retrace your steps back to the junction and keep ahead to the point where the road bends left. Leave it here and continue along **Pickets Lane**, passing several houses. Beyond them take the track out across open farmland and eventually you join a lane on a bend.

3 Go straight on, avoiding a turning for **Littlestoke House** and, on reaching the entrance to **Littlestoke Manor**, take the path by the main gate, signposted '**South Stoke 1 mile**'. Cross the field to a stile and footbridge and continue on the grassy path towards the railway line. Pass through the railway tunnel, known as the **Bogey Hole**, and cross the field, keeping woodland on the right. Exit the pasture, pass some houses and turn right at the road. Soon it bends left and leads into **South Stoke**. The pub is further along on the left, beyond the church.

Places of interest nearby

Founded in 1956 by Gilbert Beale and dedicated to the memory of his parents, **Beale Park** offers fun and entertainment for the whole family. There is a variety of water and pleasure gardens, and the park is home to many exotic birds, including flamingos, and animals such as the alpaca, ring-tailed lemur, red-necked wallaby and the dwarf zebra. Beale Park is north-west of Pangbourne on the A329.
☎ *0870 777 7160.*

7 Goring

The Catherine Wheel

The end of **Ferry Lane**, close to the start of this lovely walk, marks the spot where the Ridgeway and the Icknield Way once crossed the Thames at a ford. The routes originally formed a prehistoric trade road between East Anglia and Dorset. The ford was of vital importance to the Romans and it led to a raised causeway here. Settlements were established in the vicinity of the crossing point and during the Anglo-Saxon period the river assumed the role of a vital frontier. Streatley, on the Berkshire bank, formed part of Wessex, while Goring was in Mercia. The latter village is a very different place today, as is its neighbour. Both are smart and prosperous and both are communities especially popular with large numbers of commuters. At one time these charming riverside villages were affectionately known by train travellers as 'Boring and Discreetly'. This delightful circular route begins by heading downstream to Gatehampton Manor.

The Thames Valley

Distance – 3 miles.

OS Explorer 171 Chiltern Hills West, Henley-on-Thames & Wallingford. GR 599807.
Beginning in the centre of Goring, the walk crosses level ground beside the Thames before returning to the start along a concrete track and then a tarmac road.

Starting point Fee-paying car park behind the Catherine Wheel in Goring.

How to get there From Oxford or Wallingford follow either the A329 or the B4009 south to Goring. From the main street turn into Manor Road, then left into Station Road. The pub and adjoining car park are on the left.

The scenery is glorious as the path crosses meadows with views of the tree-fringed river meandering towards Pangbourne.

THE PUB The **Catherine Wheel** in Station Road prides itself on being the oldest pub in Goring. It is certainly an ancient building, and with its small windows and timber-framed walls looks more like a chocolate-box cottage than a village inn. The lengthy and impressive menu includes a range of light bite bar snacks and gourmet burgers. Main courses range from rib-eye steak and spaghetti bolognaise to cottage pie and vegetarian sausage and mash. There is also an extensive choice of pizzas, which you can eat in or take away. Real ales include Brakspear Special and Ordinary and Hook Norton Mild.

Open 11 am to 11 pm between Monday and Saturday, and 12 noon until 10.30 pm on Sunday.
☎ *01491 872379*

1 From the public car park next to the pub follow the path through to the **High Street** and turn left. Pass **Manor Road** and the village hall and then take the path down to the **Thames riverbank**. The next leg of the walk coincides with a section of the **Thames Path**. Follow the national trail to the left, passing lines of luxury cabin cruisers moored along this stretch. Continue along the towpath, pass a ruined boathouse and avoid a path on the left. Keep ahead beside the river, walking through a pretty tunnel of trees. Beyond it you cross several meadows, curving to the left now on the approach to a railway bridge spanning the river.

2 Pass beneath Brunel's busy railway and follow the path towards **Gatehampton Manor**. When the **Thames Path** approaches a house with a slate roof, walk away from the riverbank and cut between paddocks. Turn left at the next path junction, follow the bridleway and soon you join a concrete track. Follow it ahead as it becomes a tarmac road.

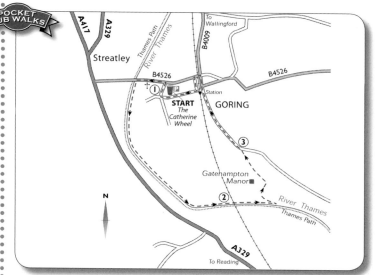

The Thames Valley

The River Thames at Goring.

3. Keep left at the next T-junction and make for the houses of **Goring**. Soon you reach the railway station and beyond it the **Queen's Arms**. Take the next turning on the left, cross the railway bridge and then turn left into **Red Cross Road**. Turn right at the next junction and follow the road along to the **Catherine Wheel**. The car park is next door to it.

Places of interest nearby

South of Goring along the A329 lies **Basildon Park**. Built to the designs of John Carr and now in the care of the National Trust, this late 18th-century house was used as one of the major locations in the latest film adaptation of Jane Austen's classic *Pride and Prejudice*. Basildon Park is 'Netherfield' in the movie and both interior and exterior scenes were shot here.
☎ *01494 755558.*

The Swan

In 1919 when **D.H. Lawrence** and his wife were renting a cottage in the village, he recorded his feelings as: 'Pleasant house, hate Pangbourne, nothing happens.' At that time the area was especially popular with artists, writers and weekend anglers. Close to the start of this fascinating walk are seven very distinctive villas known as the 'Seven Deadly Sins'. The houses were built by D.H. Evans, who founded the famous West End department store just before the turn of the 20th century though no one knows for sure why he chose as many as seven. Some theories suggest he wanted to live in a different villa each day of the week while other sources indicate he intended them for his seven mistresses. Society hostess Lady Cunard bought one of the Seven Deadly Sins early in the 20th century. Percy Stone,

Distance – 4½ miles.

OS Explorer 159 Reading, Wokingham & Pangbourne. GR 634765.
The walk begins with a glorious stretch of the Thames between Pangbourne and Basildon. Climb out of the valley to Pangbourne College and return to the start by the Pang.

Starting point There are limited parking spaces at the Swan so please use the fee-paying public car park a couple of minutes' walk from the pub.

How to get there Approach Pangbourne on either the A329 (the Reading/Wantage road) or the A340 from the south. The public car park is on the A329 just south of the railway bridge and the pub is a short distance to the north on the other side of the road.

a local resident, claimed her parties were wild and riotous, adding 'anything would have seemed wild compared to life in Pangbourne.'

From the Seven Deadly Sins the walk heads out of the valley, passing close to Pangbourne Naval College, with its famous chapel and Falklands War memorial window, before descending to the banks of the Pang, one of Berkshire's prettiest rivers.

THE PUB The **Swan** at Pangbourne is another ancient pub strongly associated with those *Three Men in a Boat*. So much has been written about this literary masterpiece that I would prefer to dwell on some lesser-known aspects of the pub's history. For example, did you know that it once represented the county boundary between Berkshire and Oxfordshire? The licensing laws differed either side of the line and closing time would vary by as much as half an hour. Keen regulars simply moved from one county to the other, taking their drink into the adjoining bar to resume imbibing. House burger, ploughman's lunch and soup of the day are among the popular favourites on the Swan's menu, and there is also fresh haddock, lasagne, bangers and mustard mash, steak and ale pie and traditional Sunday roast. Greene King IPA, Abbot Ale and Morland Speckled Hen are among the real ales.

Open 10 am until 11 pm between Sunday and Thursday, and 10 am until 12 midnight on Friday and Saturday.
☎ *0118 984 4494*

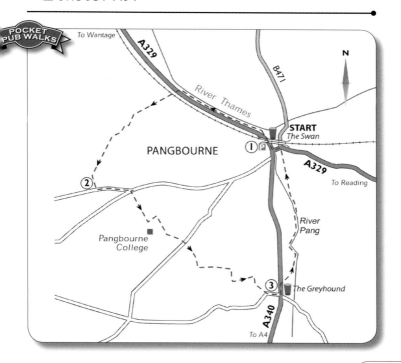

The Seven Deadly Sins.

1 From the public car park turn left, pass beneath the railway bridge and follow **Shooters Hill**. The **Swan** comes into view on the right now. Continue along the pavement beside the road and at length, on the left, you will come to the **Seven Deadly Sins**. Keep along the road to a layby and look for a path on the left. Take the path, pass under the railway line and veer left, following a winding path up through the woods to a wrought iron gate. Continue ahead, keeping the field perimeter on your left. Go diagonally across the next field to a gap in the trees and hedge and keep the field perimeter on your left as you head for the road.

2 Turn left and walk along to the next main junction. Cross over and take the drive to **Pangbourne College**, passing some tennis courts. Turn left at the T-junction, then sharp right at the next waymark. Swing left at the fork by some corrugated buildings and follow the track down to a house called **Rivendell**. Continue to the next road. Cross it and follow the track ahead to a house called **Spindleberry**. Join a path at this point and follow it across fields and open downland, eventually merging with another track on the outskirts of **Tidmarsh**. Go through a kissing gate, turn left and follow the lane down to the junction by the **Greyhound pub**.

3 Turn left, passing **Strachey Close**, which takes its name from the noted biographer and member of the Bloomsbury Group, Lytton Strachey, who lived at Tidmarsh. Now turn right to join an enclosed footpath. On reaching the entrance to **Longbridge**, swing left, avoid the turning on the left and follow the tarmac drive towards three houses. Make for two adjacent stiles ahead, take the one on the right and join the **Pang riverbank**. Cross another stile and follow the river to the footbridge. Cross over and follow the footpath across the meadows, back into **Pangbourne**. Turn left at the junction in the centre of the village, then right at the next roundabout and return to the car park.

Places of interest nearby

Moor Copse Nature Reserve is just south of Tidmarsh, off the A340. (It can be reached via an access road immediately to the north of the M4, beyond which is a small car park. A path leads to the reserve.) It is in the care of the Berks, Bucks and Oxon Wildlife Trust and is well worth visiting. Several paths allow you to explore the reserve on foot and, with the aid of several information boards, you can learn all about the vital role it plays in the cycle of nature. The River Pang runs through this area and it is commonly accepted that this delightful stretch of the river inspired the writer Kenneth Grahame to pen *The Wind in the Willows*, published in 1908. Grahame spent much of his early life in Pangbourne, staying with relatives. He returned to the village in 1924, this time making his home there, and died in 1932.

The Fisherman's Cottage

This is more a heritage trail than a walk. Reading may not enjoy the best press in the world but away from the busy roads and shopping centres there is a wealth of historic landmarks and fascinating sites to explore on foot. Starting on the Kennet and Avon Canal, the walk soon reaches the River Thames. From here one can see View Island, one of the walk's major features. Access is via the bridge at Caversham Lock and once across you can study the information boards and learn all about this wonderfully green corner of the town. View Island was once a dilapidated boatyard though you wouldn't know it to look at it today, when it is characterised by peaceful grassy expanses and a fascinating array of flora and fauna. Make for Forbury Gardens and here you can exercise your imagination by picturing the crowds as they gathered on the little hill in an effort to spot the very first train arriving at Reading station in March 1840. Beyond Forbury Gardens you find the crumbling remains of Reading Abbey and just round the corner is Reading Gaol where Reading's most famous resident, Oscar Wilde, languished for 18 months in the 1890s.

THE PUB Built as a private house and occupying a very attractive canalside location in the heart of Reading, the **Fisherman's Cottage** has almost certainly been a pub for nearly 200 years. In all probability it became a hostelry to cater for bargees and others who made their living on the water. From inside, there are good views of all the bustling activity on the canal.

Distance – 4½ miles.

OS Explorer 159 Reading, Wokingham & Pangbourne. GR 726735. Preferably, take a good street map of Reading in addition to the OS Explorer map.
Around every corner there is something new and surprising on this informative and entertaining town trail.

Starting point The Fisherman's Cottage in Orts Road.

How to get there From Reading town centre and the station area, head east along first Forbury Road then King's Road. On the left is the Prudential building. Turn left into Orts Road and follow it to the far end, then veer left into Canal Way. The pub and car park are on the left. For those not patronising the pub, alternative parking can be found at Reading station or in the town centre.

The inn's appeal widened in the mid-1980s with the addition of a light and airy conservatory. Beers range from Fuller's ESB to Gales HSB and for lager drinkers there is a choice of Stella Artois, Foster's and Carlsberg. Scampi and chicken fillet burger feature on the menu, with jacket potatoes and sandwiches.

Open 12 noon until 11 pm from Sunday to Thursday; 12 noon until midnight on Friday and Saturday.
☎ *0118 957 1553*

1 From the pub turn right and walk along the **Kennet and Avon Canal towpath**. Pass another pub – the **Jolly Anglers** – and look for a plaque on the wall of the second railway bridge as you approach **Kennet Mouth**. Cross **Horseshoe Bridge** and then head upstream along a very green and leafy stretch of the Thames. The foliage of **View Island** can be seen across the water. Continue by the river to **Caversham Lock**, cross over to

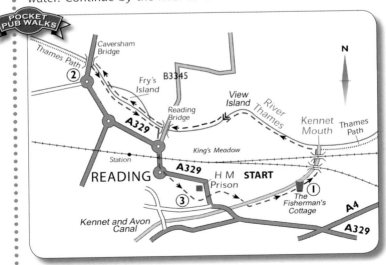

Oscar Wilde lounges in the centre of Reading.

the weir and follow a tarmac path. At the next bridge turn right to explore the island, then return to the bridge and turn right. Cross another wooden footbridge and turn sharp left. From this junction the walk heads upstream to **Reading Bridge** then on towards **Caversham Bridge**. Keep the river on your left, look for **Fry's Island** and veer to the right of the war memorial. Follow **Promenade Road** to the junction, turn left and cross **Caversham Bridge**.

2 On the far side join the southern towpath and walk back to **Reading Bridge**. Leave the river at this crossing point, go over the roundabout just near the bridge and pass beneath the railway to a second roundabout. Cross **Forbury Road** (A329) and **Forbury Gardens** are on the south side. Go diagonally across them to the **Forbury Coffee Bar**. Keep along the right-hand edge of the gardens, pass through the stone arch and go round to the right by the ruins of **Reading Abbey**. Soon you reach the **River Kennet**.

The Thames Valley

3 Turn left along **Chestnut Walk** and keep the river on your right. On the left is **Reading Gaol**. A striking image of Oscar Wilde, created to mark the centenary of his death in 2000, greets you along this stretch. Pass beneath **Forbury Road** and you cannot fail to spot the huge **Prudential building** on the opposite bank. Walk along to the next road bridge and here you have a choice. To visit the **Riverside Museum**, turn left for a short distance; to continue the walk, turn right. Make for the junction with **King's Road**, turn left and cross the **Kennet and Avon Canal**. Take the steps on the left down to the towpath and walk ahead beside the waterway, back to the pub.

Places of interest nearby

The **Riverside Museum**, part of the Bel and the Dragon pub and restaurant in Gasworks Road, tells the story of the Thames and the Kennet. Admission is free and the museum is open daily.
☎ *0118 939 9800.*

The **Museum of Reading** offers plenty of fascinating exhibitions and family attractions. Housed within Reading Town Hall, the museum has 12 interactive galleries, including exhibitions on the story of the Roman occupation of Britain and Roman Silchester.
☎ *0118 939 9800.*

The **Museum of English Rural Life** at the University of Reading houses one of this country's most informative collections of life and work in the English countryside over the last 200 years. Here you can learn all about farming through the ages, the economics and history of agriculture, land use and the environment, rural crafts and life in the countryside.
☎ *0118 378 8660.*

10 Wargrave

The Bull Hotel

Originally known as **Weregrave**, Wargrave remains one of the prettiest villages in this part of the Thames Valley. The origin of Wargrave has no connection with military cemeteries as some people mistakenly believe. Instead, the name means 'grove by the weirs'. The church dates from the First World War, replacing an earlier building which, apart from the Norman tower, was destroyed by fire on Whit Sunday 1914. Suffragettes might well have been responsible – angry because the vicar would not withdraw the word 'obey' from the marriage service. Another colourful and intriguing story associated with Wargrave involves an 18th-century Irish peer, the Earl of Barrymore. He built a theatre close to his Wargrave home and engaged the services of a famous Covent Garden clown. The opening night in 1791 was a sensation, with the cream of society in attendance. By the time he died suddenly in 1793, the Earl had frittered away more than a quarter of a million pounds on the theatre, as well as a variety of sporting pleasures. The story of the Earl of Barrymore has a final sordid footnote. The Earl was buried at Wargrave on a Sunday in order to stop his creditors seizing his body and holding it until his debts had been settled. Have a look at Wargrave's famous and historic church before you begin this delightful undulating walk in the countryside surrounding the village.

THE PUB

The **Bull Hotel** is one of Wargrave's most famous buildings. This award-winning 15th-century coaching inn in the High Street is also reputedly haunted. The story goes that the ghost of a former landlady can be heard weeping and wailing as she begs for forgiveness from her spouse after embarking on an affair and producing a child. A range of Brakspear ales is available and the restaurant menu offers the likes of breaded

Distance – 6 miles

OS Explorer 171 Chiltern Hills West, Henley-on-Thames & Wallingford. GR 786785
Dense woodland provides the backdrop for much of this delightful walk from Wargrave to picturesque Bowsey Hill and back over field paths and lanes.

Starting point The pay and display car park in School Lane off the A321 in Wargrave.

How to get there Wargrave lies on the A321 between Henley and Wokingham. School Lane can be found in the centre of the village.

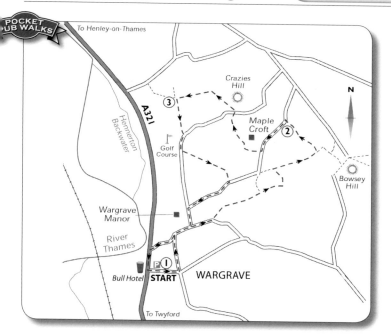

scampi, baked salmon fillet, chef's pie of the day, Cumberland sausages, chef's curry of the day, hot chilli and fresh pasta. Sandwiches and baguettes are available at lunchtime.

Open 11 am until 3 pm and 6 pm until 11 pm from Monday to Saturday; 12 noon until 4.30 pm and 7 pm until 10.30 pm on Sunday.
Telephone: 0118 940 3120

1 From the public car park turn left, then left again into **Dark Lane**. On reaching the junction with **Wargrave Hill**, turn right and pass one of the entrances to **Wargrave Manor**, ignoring a turning for **Crazies Hill** on the left. Join a path on the left just

The church of St Mary, Wargrave.

beyond **Purfield Drive**, passing through a kissing gate. Follow the obvious field path ahead, pass alongside trees to cross a footbridge and avoid a path immediately on the left. Continue towards the corner of the pasture and veer right through a hedge gap just before woodland. Turn immediately left and skirt the field, heading for two stiles and a waymark in the corner. Keep ahead on the path and after about 80 yards look for a waymark. Turn left and walk through the woods, climbing steps to turn right at the next obvious path junction. Follow the woodland path for some time and take the first left turning at the next major intersection. This is **Bowsey Hill**. Follow the path to the road and turn left.

2 Cut between trees and hedgerows, pass the entrance to **Maple Croft** on the right and watch for a stile on the right about 60

yards beyond the turning. There are two waymarked paths here. Take the one on the right, veer right to join a track and follow it to a gateway. On reaching a private sign, keep ahead for a few steps to the next gate where you will find a reassuring waymark. Keep ahead through the trees to a stile and gate and go straight over into the field. Follow the right-hand perimeter, heading for a bungalow in the corner. Skirt the garden and turn right at the road, then bear sharp left after several paces to follow a bridleway, heading downhill through the trees.

3 When you come to a path crossing the route, turn left and head up the steep slope. Negotiate several stiles before reaching the road where you turn right. Pass the drive to **Hennerton Golf Club** and take the next field path on the left. Follow it to a fence and veer right to the road. Turn right, then left at the T-junction and right at the next intersection. Follow **Wargrave Hill** down to the A321 and turn left, then left again along **School Lane** back to the car park where the walk began. The **Bull**, which you can glimpse from **School Lane**, is just a minute's walk from the car park, beside the crossroads in the village centre.

Places of interest nearby

Greys Court, north of Rotherfield Greys to the west of Henley, is well worth a visit during the summer season. The present National Trust house is gabled and of brick and flint construction. Greys Court and the village owe their name to Lord de Grey, who fought at Crécy and became one of the original Knights of the Garter. A Tudor donkey-wheel well house and the Archbishop's Maze, whose design is based on the theme of reconciliation, are fascinating features of the property.
☎ *01491 628529.*

The Flower Pot

Situated **amidst Berkshire's lush meadows** and buried deep down winding country lanes, the little village of Aston is worthy of inspection. There was once a ferry crossing at this point and a little way upstream is Temple Island, site of an elegant Georgian folly. The island also marks the start of the Henley Regatta course. The first Royal Regatta was held in June 1839 and this colourful occasion has been an important event in the town's social calendar ever since.

A sizeable chunk of the Thames Valley is seen on this glorious walk – the winding river epitomising the charm and gentle beauty of southern England.

THE PUB With its Victorian character still intact, the **Flower Pot** recalls images of Jerome K. Jerome and *Three Men in a Boat*. The building dates back to 1890 and came into being to cater for boating parties and fishermen. It remains one of the best-known pubs on this stretch of the Thames and draws many hikers following the Thames Path. Lamb shank, lasagne, half a roast chicken and sausage, egg and chips feature on the menu, together with lunchtime snacks, which include baguettes, sandwiches, ploughman's and various jacket potatoes. Brakspear Special and Bitter, Hook Norton, Stella Artois and Strongbow are available at the bar.

Open Monday to Friday from 11 am to 3 pm and 6 pm to 12 midnight; Saturday 11 am until 12 midnight; Sunday 12 noon until 11 pm.
☎ *01491 574721*

Distance – 3 miles.

OS Explorer 171 Chiltern Hills West, Henley-on-Thames & Wallingford. GR 785842.
Some of the loveliest views of the Thames can be enjoyed on this classic walk in the countryside to the south-east of Aston.

Starting point The Flower Pot at Aston.

How to get there Aston is about 1 mile north of the A4130. The lane to the village is signposted from the main road at Remenham Hill to the east of Henley and the pub is on the left in Ferry Lane, not far from the point where the road finishes at the riverbank.

The Thames Valley

1 From the pub walk back up **Aston Lane**, avoiding the route of the **Thames Path** on the left. This represents the final stage of this walk. Continue on the road, passing **Highway Cottage** on the right. Ignore a path on the right and keep ahead as the lane climbs gently out of the valley. Follow it between banks, hedgerows and trees and at length you reach a row of houses on the left. Disregard a path on the right and continue along the lane almost to the junction with the main A4130. Just before it is a stile in the left boundary, which you cross. Go diagonally across to a stile to the left of a line of conifers. Cross it and walk ahead, with a line of houses and gardens on the right. Over to the left are distant views of the **Thames Valley**. Make for

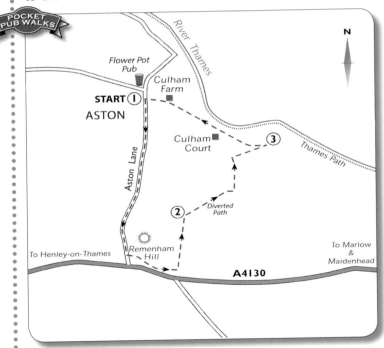

The Henley Regatta course near Aston.

the field corner and at the waymark, turn left. Follow the track towards the valley, bearing right into the next field when you reach a waymark.

2 Go through the gate and head down the field slope following the clear waymarks. Standing out among the trees on the far side of the valley is **Danesfield House**, requisitioned by the government during the Second World War and used as an RAF base. It is now a luxury hotel. Make for a gate, turn left and follow the tarmac drive. On reaching a fork, keep left towards **Culham Court** and as you approach a cattle-grid and a gate, veer right to follow the signposted path. Cut between trees, with deer fencing on the left, and then follow the path across several fields to reach the route of the **Thames Path**.

3 Turn left and when the path splits, keep left on the main public footpath. Continue ahead, passing **Culham Court** on the left, and negotiate several kissing gates before reaching a sizeable field. A lengthy sweep of the river is seen from this wonderful vantage point. Cross the pasture towards **Culham Farm**, go through the gate to a **Thames Path** sign and follow the track through the trees to the road. Turn right and return to the **Flower Pot**, just a few yards away.

Places of interest nearby

The **River and Rowing Museum** at Henley provides great entertainment – especially if the weather becomes unsettled. The fascinating history of Britain's rowing heritage is illustrated here, and there are permanent galleries, absorbing exhibitions, unique interactive displays and plenty of children's activities to keep you fully occupied. There is even an audio-guide to the timeless classic *The Wind in the Willows*.
☎ *01491 415600.*

The King's Head

Children's writers come and go but one author is still a household name 40 years after her death. Enid Blyton, who, in the 1920s and 30s, lived at Old Thatch adjacent to the Spade Oak pub, directly on the route of this walk, was a prolific writer who created a magical fantasy world of innocence and adventure for children. Through her work she has left us a wonderful legacy and those of us of a certain age who read her books avidly as youngsters now look upon her stories with a very real sense of nostalgia. Blyton's output is staggering. She published more than 600 books, with Noddy, the Famous Five and the Secret Seven among her best-known and best-loved characters.

This short but varied walk begins by exploring one of the *Midsomer Murder* villages. The church and cottages at Little

The Thames Valley

Distance – 2½ miles.

OS Explorer 172 Chiltern Hills East, High Wycombe, Maidenhead & Rickmansworth. GR 873842.
Water is very much the theme of this walk. Former gravel pits transformed into large lakes and a scenic stretch of the Thames above Bourne End are the key features.

Starting point The King's Head, Little Marlow.

How to get there Take the A404 between junction 8/9 of the M4 and High Wycombe and turn off eastwards on the A4155 towards Bourne End. The turning for Little Marlow is on the right. The pub is also on the right.

Marlow are easily recognisable as classic English village locations in the long-running detective series on ITV. From here the route is through woods and across meadows to the banks of the Thames. Downstream near Bourne End, the walk reaches Spade Oak Wharf, once owned by the former nunnery at Little Marlow. During the Middle Ages this was an important stop for river traffic. It would have been used by the nuns receiving goods from London.

THE PUB The 17th-century **King's Head** at Little Marlow has some charming features. For example – the ceilings and walls of the bars are oak beamed and there are open fires to draw you in on a cold winter's day, as well as a delightful garden to enjoy in warmer weather. Expect to see plenty of walkers here as the pub is only a relatively short walk from the Thames Path. The menu includes sandwiches and jacket potatoes and also offers a choice of hearty main courses, such as pheasant casserole, lamb shank and stir-fry duck with plum sauce. Real ales range from Timothy Taylor Landlord to Fuller's London Pride.

Open 11 am to 11 pm on Monday and Saturday and 12 noon to 10.30 pm on Sunday.
☎ *01628 484407*

1 Turn right on leaving the pub and pass the village cricket ground on the left. Avoid a turning on the right for the **Queen's Head** and continue through the village. Carry on to the heart of **Little Marlow** and look for the village church nestling in the corner of the main square. Ahead of you is the north-facing, timber-framed elevation of **Manor Farm** and on the left is the **Old Vicarage**. Continue at the private road sign and pass over a brook. Ignore a footpath on the left, representing the return leg of the walk, and keep ahead, passing a row of houses on the right. Soon you come to the site of sewage treatment works;

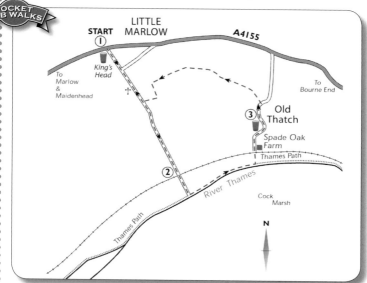

Spade Oak Wharf on the Thames.

keep ahead to several cottages and a redbrick house and begin following a woodland path. Several lakes, once gravel pits, loom into view on the left as you pass between the trees. At length you reach a railway track.

2 This is the Marlow to Bourne End branch line. Cross it with care and continue ahead across a meadow to reach the **Thames riverbank**. In the corner, by a sign for **Spade Oak Meadow**, turn left through a gate and follow the **Thames Path** downstream. Various houses, villas and single-storey dwellings are seen on the opposite bank of the river. When there is a break in the row, with the buildings of **Bourne End** seen ahead on a curve of the river, go through a kissing gate to reach **Spade Oak Wharf**. A notice states that the land here has been purchased for 'the quiet enjoyment of the public'. Avoid the **Thames Path** as it continues beside the river and turn left at this point. Re-cross the Marlow to Bourne End railway and pass **Spade Oak Farm** on

the right. Continue on the road and pass a car park on the left just before the **Spade Oak pub**.

3 Next door is **Old Thatch**, the former home of Enid Blyton. At this point look for a footpath on the left. Follow it briefly to a galvanised kissing gate, turn right and keep parallel to the road. Cross a footbridge and as you approach the road again swing left into trees. Pass between them to reach the edge of a field and at this point veer left along its boundary. Continue for some time on this path, following it between fields and woodland. Go through a gate, cross an access road to the gravel pits and continue on the footpath over the next pasture. Cross a footbridge and follow the path beside a brook to reach a more substantial bridge. Curve to the right shortly after the bridge and now the church at **Little Marlow** can be seen among the trees. On reaching the lane, turn right and retrace your steps to the pub.

Places of interest nearby

The garden of **Old Thatch** is open to the public between 11 am and 5 pm on Saturday and Sunday and bank holidays between late May and the end of August. Please note that the house is private.
☎ *01628 527518.*

Marlow is one of those towns that cries out to be discovered on foot. Shelley lived here in the early 19th century, the town's suspension bridge was completed in 1832 by William Tierney Clark, who was inspired by similar bridges he had seen in London and Budapest, and the historic Compleat Angler Hotel is where *The Flying Swan*, one of the early television soaps, was filmed in the mid-1960s. For futher details, contact Marlow Tourist Information Centre.
☎ *01628 483597.*

13 Cookham

The Bel and the Dragon

The name of one unique man remains inextricably linked with the Thameside village of Cookham – that of the artist Stanley Spencer. A controversial figure, Spencer, who died in 1959, is still the subject of speculation and debate. He was born in Cookham High Street in 1891 and spent most of his life in Cookham. The former Methodist chapel in the village is now a gallery devoted to his work. Officially opened in 1962, the newly refurbished exhibition space houses many of Spencer's

Distance – 4½ miles

OS Explorer 172 Chiltern Hills East, High Wycombe, Maidenhead & Rickmansworth, GR 894853.
A lengthy stretch by the Thames before the path crosses Cock Marsh to begin a steep climb to a memorable viewpoint east of Winter Hill.

Starting point The free car park on Cookham Moor.

How to get there Cookham lies about 3½ miles north of Maidenhead on the A4094. Turn west into the High Street (B4447) and the entrance to the car park on Cookham Moor is on the right.

paintings, including *The Last Supper* and the view of *Cookham from Englefield*. Spencer often used Cookham as the backdrop to many of his paintings. If time permits, have a look at the village before you start the walk and even when you do get into your stride, it's worth lingering a little in the vicinity of Holy Trinity church, parts of which date from the 12th century. The church includes a number of monuments and brasses – particularly memorable is the huge 15th-century tower. A few hundred yards away is Cookham Bridge, built in 1867 and replacing an earlier wooden structure of 1840. It came to be known as 'the cheapest bridge across the Thames' and there was a toll in operation until the late 1940s.

THE PUB The **Bel and the Dragon** in Cookham High Street is one of the oldest licensed houses in the country and it's a cosy and inviting place with an open fireplace and wooden tables. Fuller's London Pride, Brakspear Bitter and Courage Best feature among the beers, while the imaginative and extensive menu offers such dishes as beer-battered fillet of haddock with handcut chips, calves' liver with crispy pancetta, and trio of Cumberland sausages. Sandwiches and baguettes are also available.

Open from 11.30 am to 11 pm between Monday and Saturday and 12 noon to 10.30 pm on Sunday.
☎ *01628 521263*

1 From the parking area on **Cookham Moor** turn left and walk along the **High Street**, passing a variety of shops, pubs and cottages. On the left here is the **Bel and the Dragon**. Turn left at the next junction with the A4094 towards **Marlow**. On the right here is the **Tarry Stone** around which sports were once played. The sarsen boulder occupied different positions in the village until transferred to its present setting in 1937. Shortly you come to a turning for **Cookham church** on the left. Take it and walk through the churchyard, passing **Stanley Spencer's**

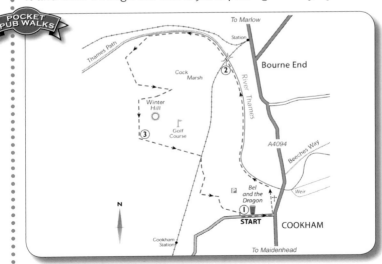

The Tarry Stone at Cookham.

grave on the left. Follow the **Thames Path** and on reaching the riverbank, turn left and head upstream, passing a boatyard and a pub before eventually reaching the edge of **Cock Marsh**.

Now in the care of the National Trust, the marsh includes four bowl barrows or prehistoric burial mounds, the largest of which has a circumference of 90 feet. When excavated in the 19th century it was found that two of the barrows contained early Bronze Age burials dating back 4,000 years.

Continue along the riverside path and you will see the steep chalk escarpment of **Winter Hill** in the distance.

2 Walk on beside the **Thames**, pass a railway bridge carrying the Maidenhead to Bourne End line and go through several gates to reach a solitary white cottage near the river. Look for the footpath sign, take the track ahead and when you reach a concrete track on a bend, turn left and cross the field towards the escarpment. Pass through a kissing gate to reach a junction

The Thames Valley

of paths. Turn left here and follow the path to a waymark. Swing sharp right here, heading diagonally up the steep escarpment. Keep right when you reach the top and head west. Keep an eye out for a kissing gate over in the left-hand bank, go through it and follow the field path ahead.

3 As you approach a mock Tudor house turn left to join a footpath, passing to the left of the property. Cross **Winter Hill golf course**, keeping to the left of a corrugated store, and pass a bunker. Aim for the railway ahead, cross the bridge spanning it and turn right immediately beyond it. Look for a seat and, at the end of the golf course, continue ahead on a track. As you approach a road, turn sharp left by several houses, one of which is called **Fiveways**. Follow the path down to a kissing gate, keep right and return to the car park on **Cookham Moor**.

Places of interest nearby

Winter Hill and **Quarry Wood** are perfect for exploring on foot. The former offers magnificent views over the Thames Valley while the latter is where Kenneth Grahame used to walk as a child. In fact, it is said that while out roaming this beech woodland, he was inspired to write about the 'wild wood' in his classic story for children *The Wind in the Willows*. To reach them from Cookham, head towards Maidenhead on the B4447. Branch right for Cookham station and Cookham Dean and then make for Winter Hill where there is a viewpoint and parking beside the road.

Burnham Beeches, due east of Cookham across the Thames, is a National Nature Reserve covering 600 acres. Within its boundaries is the world's largest collection of ancient beech, with an average age of more than 300 years. To appreciate its unique character and beauty, either take a drive through the reserve or explore it on foot.

The Dumb Bell

Isambard **Kingdom Brunel**, born in 1806, our best-known and most talented engineer, did more to change the face of the British landscape than anyone else. It simply isn't possible to travel very far in this country without stumbling upon examples of his fine work. With his railways, docks, bridges and viaducts, he has left us a lasting legacy. This Victorian genius left his mark in the Thames Valley too and nowhere is this better represented than in the closing stages of this memorable and very enjoyable riverside walk, which starts just outside Maidenhead. It was here that Brunel was faced with the daunting challenge of getting his

Distance – 3½ miles.

OS Explorer 172 Chiltern Hills East, High Wycombe, Maidenhead & Rickmansworth and 160 Windsor, Weybridge & Bracknell. GR 906813.

A fascinating walk, which combines a man-made flood channel with Britain's greatest river and concludes by passing beneath one of Brunel's most famous railway bridges.

Starting point The Dumb Bell pub on the A4 at Maidenhead.

How to get there *From Maidenhead follow the A4 to the town's eastern outskirts and the pub is on the left just beyond a turning for Taplow, also on the left.*

broad-gauge West Country line to span both the River Thames and the adjacent towpath. Typically, he found a way to overcome the problem. In 1839 he designed a railway bridge that is still celebrated as an awesome engineering achievement today. Before reaching this lasting monument to Brunel's achievements, the walk meanders along the river, offering splendid views of the picturesque and highly desirable village of Bray over on the far bank.

THE PUB The **Dumb Bell** has a smart interior and offers an extensive choice of meals, snacks and drinks. Among the main dishes are spit roasted chicken, fish and chips, scampi, and spicy bean burger. Lighter fare includes a selection of sandwiches, with fillings that include tuna mayonnaise and bacon, lettuce and tomato, and a range of jacket potatoes. Ales are likely to be Morland Old Speckled Hen and Tetley; Amstel German beer is also a popular favourite.

Open 11.30 am until 11 pm on Monday to Saturday; 11.30 am to 10.30 pm on Sunday.
☎ *01628 630817*

1 From the pub turn right for about 100 yards to some traffic lights and then swing left at the sign for **Taplow Lake** and the **Jubilee River Way**. Pass beneath a railway bridge and then beside a rather striking stone cottage on the right. Keep ahead on the tarmac lane and an assortment of boats might be seen over by the water's edge as **Taplow Lake** edges into view. Continue ahead to a bridge spanning the **Jubilee River flood channel** and turn

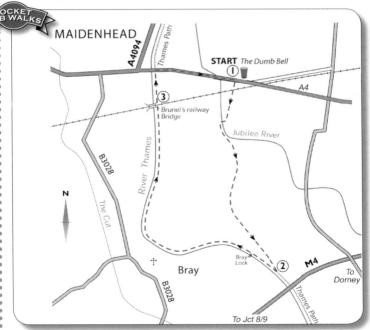

The Thames Valley

Brunel's famous railway bridge at Maidenhead.

right to cross it. As you do so, look to the right for a striking view of the railway with the outline of **Taplow Court** on the horizon. Once over the bridge bear left and follow the bridleway along the banks of the **Jubilee River**, a fledgling waterway compared with the nearby Thames. Keep to the track as it veers away from the water, still following the bridleway. Continue between fields and alongside trees and, on reaching a junction, keep ahead on the bridleway towards **Amerden Cottage**, avoiding a footpath on the right. Pass the cottage and cut between trees.

2 When the track bends left by **Amerden Lodge**, turn right to follow the footpath for a few paces to the banks of the **Thames**. Turn right and follow the towpath at **Bray Lock**. Beyond it continue along the path between farmland and the river. Along this stretch the outline of **Bray church** looms into view and very

soon you are looking across the river to the houses and cottages of this most exclusive of riverside villages. Notice where the lane reaches the riverbank on the other side – this marks the site of an old ferry crossing. Draw level with the church and continue beside the river, with good views across to rows of imposing waterside villas with gardens running down to the Thames. On reaching the entrance to a house called **Harefield** on the right, walk ahead as directed by a waymark and follow the drive towards Brunel's famous bridge.

The bridge's brick arches are the widest and flattest in the world, with each span measuring 128 feet with a rise of only 24 feet. Its graceful lines and elegant symmetry were expertly captured by Turner in his renowned painting 'Rain, Steam and Speed'.

3 Along here you can spot the road bridge through the right-hand railway arch. Continue along the road beyond the railway bridge and when you reach the road bridge, turn right and follow the pavement back to the pub.

Places of interest nearby

Maidenhead is worth exploring on foot. Among its best-known features is **Boulter's Lock**, just upstream from Brunel's railway bridge. During the Edwardian era this was a fashionable spot on the river. Contact Maidenhead Tourist Information Centre for more on the town.
☎ *01628 796502.*

The Waterman's Arms

One world-famous landmark stands head and shoulders above Windsor and represents the theme to this very varied riverside walk. Windsor Castle's dominant Round Tower was built by Henry II and is visible for miles around. The flag flies from the tower when the Queen is in residence and these days that is for much of the time. Our much-loved monarch regards Windsor as her favourite royal residence.

The walk begins by crossing Windsor Bridge, erected in 1822. Until the beginning of the 20th century there was a toll here – the living were required to pay the princely sum of 2d while the departed could be carried across by coffin for 6/8d. The bridge was pedestrianised in 1970. Later, the route crosses Eton's famous playing fields where, according to Wellington, the Battle of Waterloo was won. With its fine, world-class reputation, Eton College remains one of this country's great institutes of learning – Gladstone described it as the 'Queen of Public Schools'.

THE PUB The **Waterman's Arms** was built about 1542 and was originally used as a plague house. Bodies were floated downriver and laid out here prior to burial. The pub is also, reputedly, haunted. A former landlord claims to have seen the

Distance – 5½ miles.

OS Explorer 160 Windsor, Weybridge & Bracknell. GR 966773.
A fine walk, which begins by following the Thames downstream towards Datchet, then makes for Eton Wick and the river again via a stretch of flood channel and Eton's renowned playing fields.

Starting point The Waterman's Arms in Brocas Street, Eton.

How to get there Eton is just to the north of Windsor (junction 6 of the M4) and is well signposted. There is no car park at the pub. However, there are spaces in both Eton and nearby Windsor. From any of the car parks (most of them are pay and display) make for Eton High Street and walk to the Windsor end where you'll find the junction with Brocas Street. The inn is along on the right.

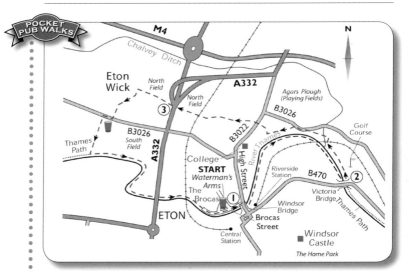

ghost of a young boy warming his hands over an open fire, even though the fireplace had been removed years before! Look above you in the bar and you'll spot the entire route of our greatest river depicted on the ceiling. What is in effect a mural is very striking and many of the river's most famous features are included. Snacks and main meals, including fresh fish and sausage, egg and chips, make up the menu. A traditional Sunday roast is also served. Large parties and special diets are catered for and there is a spacious dining area. For real ale drinkers there is a choice of beers, including Brakspear and Fuller's London Pride.

Open 11 am until 11.30 pm every day.
☎ *01753 861001*

1 From the pub walk up **Brocas Street** to the T-junction. Turn right and cross the bridge over the **Thames** to the **Windsor bank**. Turn immediately left and keep the river on your left.

Join **Romney Walk** at the end of the road and keep **Windsor Riverside station** to your right. Bear left at a tarmac drive and walk along to a boatyard. Follow the signposted **Thames Path** through the trees and along to **Black Potts railway bridge**. As you approach **Victoria Bridge**, veer over to the right and exit to the road. Turn left, cross the bridge over the river and as the road sweeps round to the right, take the left-hand path down some steps.

2 Turn left to follow the obvious path across **Datchet golf course**. Pass beneath the railway once again and then briefly follow the path alongside the **Jubilee River flood channel**, soon turning left at the first bridge. Pass through two gates on the opposite bank and keep ahead to a third gate before reaching a slipway running down to the water's edge. Keep ahead to the next road and continue to a footpath sign. Turn left here, cross a bridge and then take the path ahead across **Eton's famous playing**

Activity on the Thames.

The Thames Valley

fields. On reaching a junction of paths by a bridge, turn sharp right in front of it and then immediately swing round to the left, making for the road. Go straight across to a gate and keep ahead over playing fields to a bridge. Join a track at this point and follow it along the left-hand edge of a sports field, avoiding a footbridge on the left. Make for two brick cottages and veer left to follow the drive to a T-junction. Turn right and follow the lane, passing under the railway. Beyond it continue ahead along the narrow path, making for the Windsor relief road.

3 Pass under the road and continue ahead across fields to reach a junction of rights of way. Turn left over a stile, cross a footbridge over **Common Ditch** and turn right across the meadow, keeping roughly parallel to the ditch on your right to reach a galvanised kissing gate leading out to a lane. Turn left and follow it round to the **Greyhound pub**. Bear left here and make for the road in **Eton Wick**. Turn right, cross over and take the waymarked path over the meadows to meet the **Thames Path**. Follow the trail downstream, with the river on your right. Pass beneath the relief road and the railway and cross **The Brocas** to reach the **Waterman's Arms** where the walk began.

Places of interest nearby

Windsor is one of the most visited towns in the south and it's easy to see why. Apart from the world-famous castle, there are many other popular attractions to keep you occupied and entertained as part of your day out in the Thames Valley. If you've still plenty of energy left after your walk around Windsor and Eton, take a stroll in magnificent **Windsor Great Park**, a vast 4,800 acre area of wooded parkland and glorious landscaped gardens. Contact Windsor Tourist Information Centre for further details.
☎ *01753 743900.*